SCIENCE IDEAS IN 30 SECONDS

First published in the UK in 2014 by Ivy Kids.
This edition published in the US in 2018 by

Ivy Kids

An imprint of The Quarto Group
The Old Brewery
6 Blundell Street
London N7 9BH
United Kingdom
www.QuartoKnows.com

ISBN: 978-1-78240-609-9

This book was conceived, designed & produced by

Ivy Kids

58 West Street, Brighton BN1 2RA, United Kingdom

CREATIVE DIRECTOR	Peter Bridgewater
COMMISSIONING EDITOR	Hazel Songhurst
MANAGING EDITOR	Hazel Songhurst
PROJECT EDITOR	Cath Senker
ART DIRECTOR	Kim Hankinson
DESIGNER	Lisa McCormick
ILLUSTRATORS	Melvyn Evans (color)
	Marta Munoz (black & white)

Printed in China

1 3 5 7 9 10 8 6 4 2

SCIENCE
IDEAS
IN 30 SECONDS

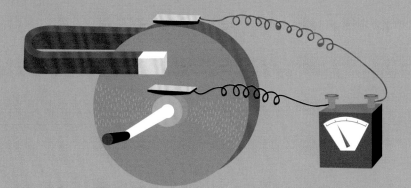

DR. MIKE GOLDSMITH

IVY KIDS

Contents

About this book
... in 60 seconds

Today, science rules the world. The clothes we wear, the food we eat, the buildings we live in, and the TV we watch all depend on scientific knowledge. Science keeps us healthy, too, and it is thanks to science that we understand so much about the universe around us.

But it hasn't always been this way. It has been less than three thousand years since anyone started to think in what we would call a scientific way.

The first such people were the ancient Greeks, who tried hard to understand how the universe really worked. Most of their ideas turned out to be wrong, partly because they did not clearly understand how science should be done. They were good at suggesting reasons for all kinds of things—from the weather to the stars and from sounds to volcanoes. Yet they did not understand that good ideas are just the starting point of good science. Careful experiments and calculations are just as important.

It was only in the sixteenth century that a modern approach to science became accepted and, from then on, progress was swift. It became faster when, in the nineteenth century, people realized that science could do more than explain how the world worked. It could show them how to build machines and make new materials. Illnesses that once killed millions of people could be cured.

As science became more useful, governments took it more seriously. In the twentieth century, large sums of money were spent on science projects, allowing greater breakthroughs to be made.

Ever since science began, it has been kept going by brilliant ideas. Thirty of the most important are explained in this book. Every topic has a page you can read to grasp the main facts—fast. If time is short, there's also a speedy sum-up. And don't forget to try out the missions and test the theories for yourself.

Ancient Greeks

The first scientific thinkers lived more than two thousand years ago in Greece. Unlike other societies before and most since, people in ancient Greece were not told what to think about the world by their religion. They were free to develop their own ideas. Beginning in about 600 BCE, Greek thinkers came up with the principles that defined science.

Ancient Greeks
Glossary

astronomy The science of things beyond Earth, including the Sun, Moon, and stars.

biology The science of living things.

chemistry The science of materials and their reactions.

compound A substance that is made by combining one or more elements. Water is a compound, made of the two elements hydrogen and oxygen.

element A substance that cannot be divided into simpler substances. Gold and iron are both elements.

ellipse An oval shape. The planets move around the Sun in ellipses.

geocentric The theory that the planets, the Sun, and the stars go around Earth.

heliocentric The theory that the Sun is the center of the universe and the planets go around it.

logic A step-by-step way of working things out using agreed rules.

nuclear To do with the nuclei (the cores in the center) of atoms.

oxygen A gas in the air that we need to breathe.

physics The study of matter and energy and the way it moves and changes.

planet A large world that moves around a star. Earth is a planet.

solar system The Sun, together with Earth, the Moon, and all the planets, comets, and other objects that move around it.

sound waves Vibrations in the air that come from a vibrating object. They cause our eardrums to vibrate, which the brain understands as sounds.

star A huge glowing ball of hot gas. The Sun is a star.

universe Everything that exists.

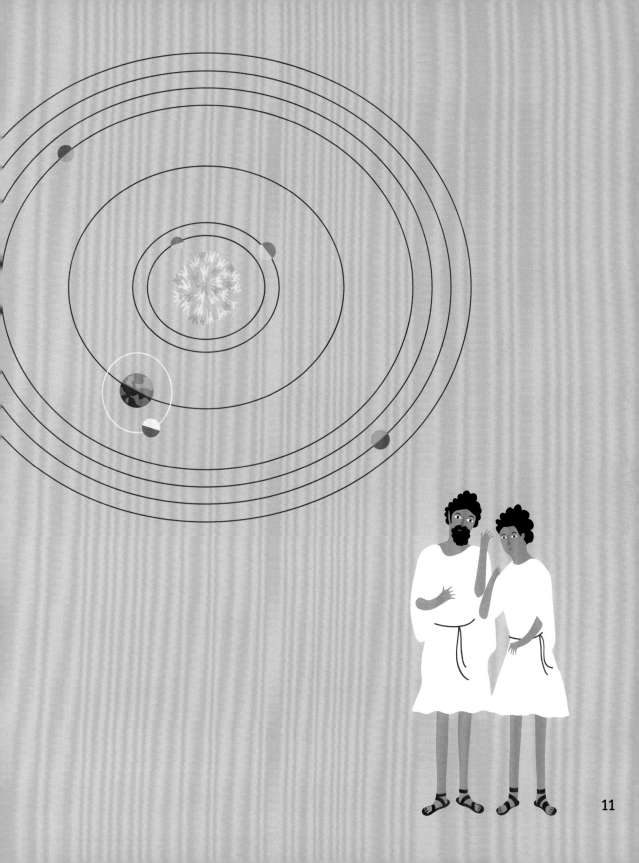

Logic

... in 30 seconds

"Science" is a method of explaining anything in the universe, and the knowledge gathered using that method. The people that came up with the method of science were the ancient Greeks. One of the most important was Aristotle, who lived about 2,300 years ago.

Almost all of Aristotle's discoveries were wrong! For example, he thought that the sun went around Earth, that stones fall because they are seeking their natural place, and that women have fewer teeth than men.

But we remember Aristotle today for his scientific method of finding things out. In his day, most people thought that the gods caused everything, from rainfall to sickness. That's really not an explanation at all. Aristotle and some other Greeks thought that the world could be explained logically.

Aristotle

Logic has been the guiding principle of science ever since. Thanks to science and scientists, we understand a lot about the universe, and we have learned to treat diseases and build incredible machines.

3-second sum-up

Science is about logical thinking.

Main Areas of Science Today

Physics The study of matter and energy and the way it moves and changes. Motion and change are caused by energy, which can take many forms, such as heat, light, and electricity.

Chemistry The study of the ways in which different kinds of matter affect each other and join to make new kinds.

Biology The study of living things.

Astronomy The study of objects beyond Earth.

Math Explains the World

... in 30 seconds

Today, every kind of science involves math, but this hasn't always been true. The scientist who first used math to explain how the world worked was Pythagoras, who lived 200 years before Aristotle.

Pythagoras discovered why two strings on a musical instrument make harmonious (pleasant) sounds when played together. He divided the length of the shorter string by the length of the longer one. He found that if the answer was a simple fraction, such as one-half or one-quarter, the sound was harmonious. The scientific reason for this is that the different sound waves mix to make a simple pattern if their lengths fit together neatly.

Pythagoras was so impressed by this discovery that he decided the whole universe could be explained through numbers and math.

Pythagoras

He was right. Today, scientists use this mathematical approach to study many kinds of waves, including sound waves, light waves, and earthquake waves. They use numbers and math to make amazing discoveries.

3-second sum-up

Math is vital to science.

3-minute mission Find the Speed of Sound

You need: • 2 saucepan lids • Tape measure • Stopwatch • A friend

Stand your friend at the edge of a large, open area. Move far away taking yard-long paces, counting them as you go. Now clash the pan lids. Your friend should start a stopwatch when they see you clash and stop when they hear it. Speed equals distance divided by time, so divide the yards you walked by the seconds they measured to find the speed of sound. Check your answer online!

Pythagoras used math to explain why sound waves in a simple pattern sound harmonious.

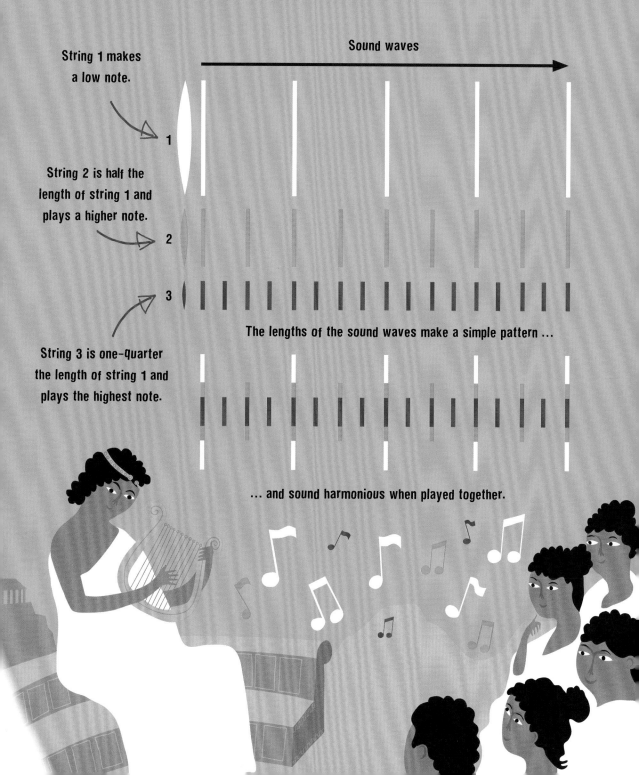

Sound waves

String 1 makes a low note.

1

String 2 is half the length of string 1 and plays a higher note.

2

3

String 3 is one-quarter the length of string 1 and plays the highest note.

The lengths of the sound waves make a simple pattern ...

... and sound harmonious when played together.

Elements

... in 30 seconds

An important idea in science is that all the things around us, from sugar to stars and seawater to burgers, are made from a much smaller number of substances called elements. This idea started with the ancient Greeks, especially Empedocles, who lived about 2,500 years ago.

Empedocles believed that there are just four elements: earth, air, fire, and water, each with special properties and a natural place. Water is naturally found above earth and below air, and is cold and wet. Fire is hot and dry and has its place above the air, so that flames burn upward.

Empedocles

Today, we know that there are about 100 elements. None of them are the four described by Empedocles. Water, for instance, is made from the elements hydrogen and oxygen. It was not until 1939 that all the naturally-occurring elements were discovered.

3-second sum-up

Every substance is made from elements.

3-minute mission Combining Elements

Iron is the most common element on Earth and many metal objects contain it. It reacts with oxygen from air to form rust, which is iron oxide. Here's how to make it:

You need: • Paper towels • Lemon juice • Salt • Small metal objects, such as nails, paper clips, pins, etc.

1 Layer some paper towels on an old tray.

2 Put some unwanted metal objects, such as nails, pins, paper clips, and nail files on the paper.

3 Mix together a few spoonfuls of lemon juice and salt. Sprinkle them over the pieces of metal.

4 In a few days, rust will appear.

Empedocles believed there were
only four elements. Today, we know
that there are about a hundred.

Fire

Earth

Empedocles' four elements were
earth, air, fire, and water.

Water

Air

We know today that air is made
of many elements and some gases,
such as carbon dioxide.

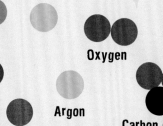

Oxygen

Argon

Carbon dioxide

Neon

Nitrogen

Solar System

... in 30 seconds

Until a few thousand years ago, it was common sense that the Sun moved around Earth, rising in the east in the morning, traveling across the sky, and setting in the west in the evening.

When it was noticed that some "stars" wandered around the sky over the year, it was decided that these too must move around Earth. They were called "planets."

Aristarchus

In about 270 BCE, a Greek called Aristarchus measured the size of the Sun. Although he didn't get it right, he proved that it is far larger than Earth. This fact probably led Aristarchus to decide that tiny Earth went around the enormous Sun.

Few agreed with Aristarchus for about 1,800 years. Then, the astronomers Copernicus, Kepler, and Galileo showed he was correct. Earth is a planet, and all the planets move around the Sun, which is a star.

3-second sum-up

All the planets travel around the Sun.

3-minute mission Draw an Ellipse

The planets travel around the Sun in ellipses (ovals).

You need: • Corkboard • Large sheet of paper • 2 push pins • 8-inch (20-cm) length of thin string • Pencil

1 Lay the paper on the board.

2 Push the pins in, near the middle, 2 inches (5 cm) apart.

3 Knot the string ends together. Loop the string around the pins. Gently pull the loop into a triangle using the pencil.

4 Keep the triangular loop taut and draw around the pins. The shape you make is an ellipse.

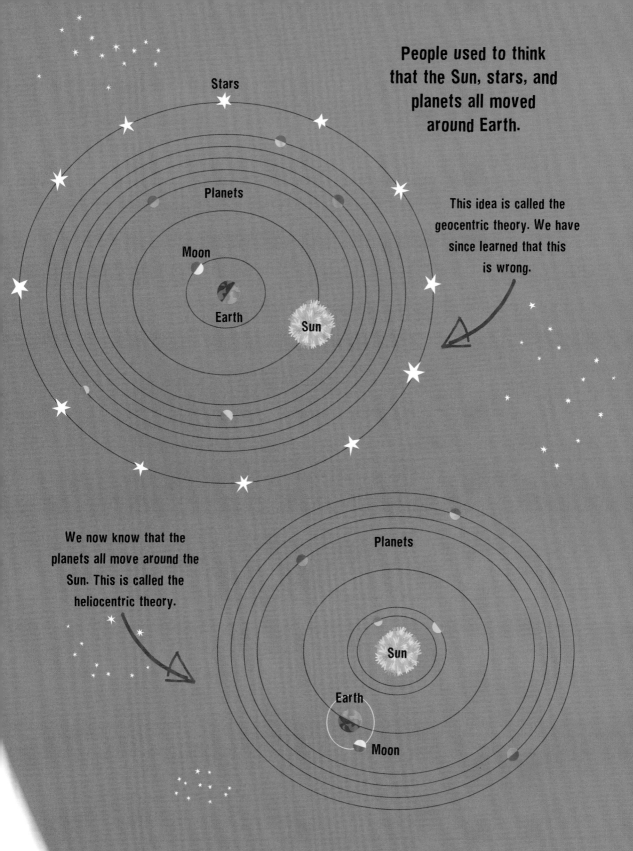

People used to think that the Sun, stars, and planets all moved around Earth.

Stars

Planets

Moon

Earth

Sun

This idea is called the geocentric theory. We have since learned that this is wrong.

We now know that the planets all move around the Sun. This is called the heliocentric theory.

Planets

Sun

Earth

Moon

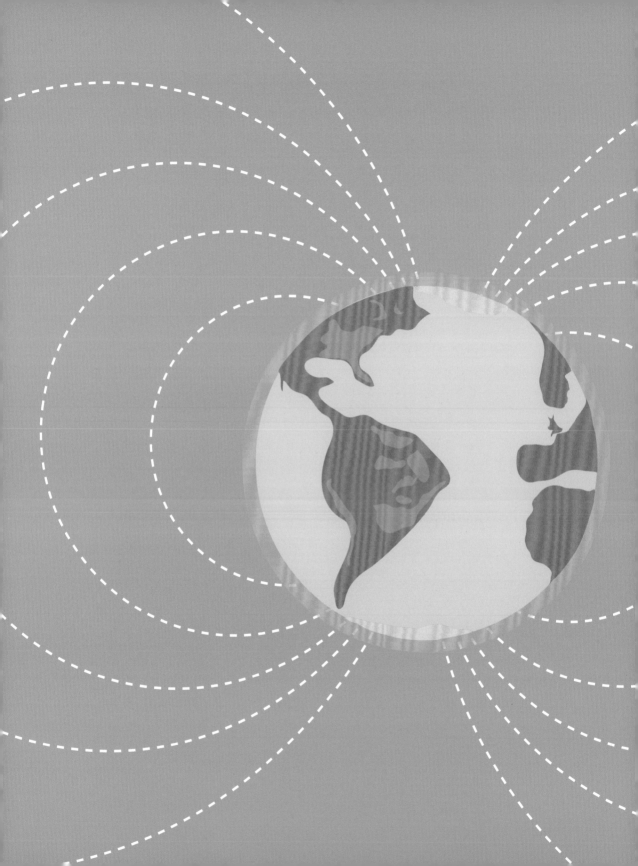

The Scientific Revolution

After the ancient Greek civilization ended in the fifth century BCE, there was little progress in science in Europe. However, scientists in the Arab world followed up on the ideas of the Greeks. In the twelfth century, Greek and Arabic scientific writings were brought to Europe, which led to new interest in science there.

The Scientific Revolution
Glossary

amber A sticky, clear, orange liquid that oozes out of some kinds of trees and then sets hard.

atom A tiny object made of a number of even tinier particles. Atoms link together to make all the things we see around us.

cell The building block from which all living things are made. Tiny living things have only one cell, but large organisms, such as humans, have trillions.

comet An object that is like an iceberg, but travels through space. Sometimes, comets travel close to the Sun, which makes them steam and shine, and then they can be seen from Earth.

compass An instrument used by travelers to find which direction they are going in. A compass contains a long, thin magnet that is free to turn around. This always lines up so that its ends point to the North and South poles of Earth.

drag The force of the air, water, or ground that acts against the movement of an aircraft or other vehicle.

electric charge An amount of electricity, which can be either positive or negative.

electric motor A device that uses a magnet to make an electric wire move. Motors are usually constructed to make a wheel spin.

electron A tiny particle. Atoms contain electrons.

force A push or pull. Gravity is a force.

friction The force that happens when one moving object comes into contact with another object. Friction slows down a moving object.

gravity The force that holds you to the ground and causes things to fall. It keeps the moon moving around Earth, and Earth moving around the Sun.

mass The amount of stuff there is in something. On Earth, the more mass a thing has, the more it weighs.

microscope An instrument used to see tiny objects clearly.

nucleus (plural: nuclei) The core in the center of something, such as a cell or an atom.

particle Any tiny lump of matter too small to see. Atoms are particles, and so are electrons.

pendulum A weight that swings freely from side to side.

planet A large world that moves around a star. Earth is a planet.

poles The two ends of something, such as Earth or a magnet.

solar system The Sun, together with Earth, the moon, and all the planets, comets, and other objects that move around it.

spectrum (plural: spectra) A rainbow-like smear of light. Spectra can be used to find out about bright objects such as stars.

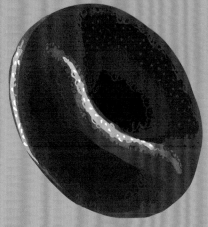

Magnetism and Electricity

... in 30 seconds

Thousands of years ago, people noticed that some rare types of rocks attract (pull) some things toward them, and some materials (such as amber) attract light objects, such as feathers, when they are rubbed. These two effects are due to magnetism and to electricity.

Magnetic objects are very useful. If they are allowed to turn around freely, they always end up with one pole (end) pointing north and the other pointing south. Magnets used like this are called compasses. In about 1600, William Gilbert showed that compasses work because Earth is a gigantic magnet.

Gilbert also experimented with electricity. Centuries later, other scientists learned how to make and control magnetism and electricity. Today, we rely on them for almost all the gadgets we use. For instance, washing machines contain motors, which use electricity and magnetism to make the drum spin.

William Gilbert

3-second sum-up

Electricity and magnetism make machinery work.

Electricity in Action

If you rub a balloon on your sweater and hold it to a wall, the balloon will stick to the wall. It will also attract shreds of paper. Why? Rubbing the balloon makes tiny particles called electrons collect on it. This "charges" the balloon with "negative" static electricity. When the balloon comes close to other objects, the electrons gathered on the balloon push away the electrons in the object. This leaves an area of "positive" charge on the object. Positive and negative charges attract each other, so the balloon and object are pulled together.

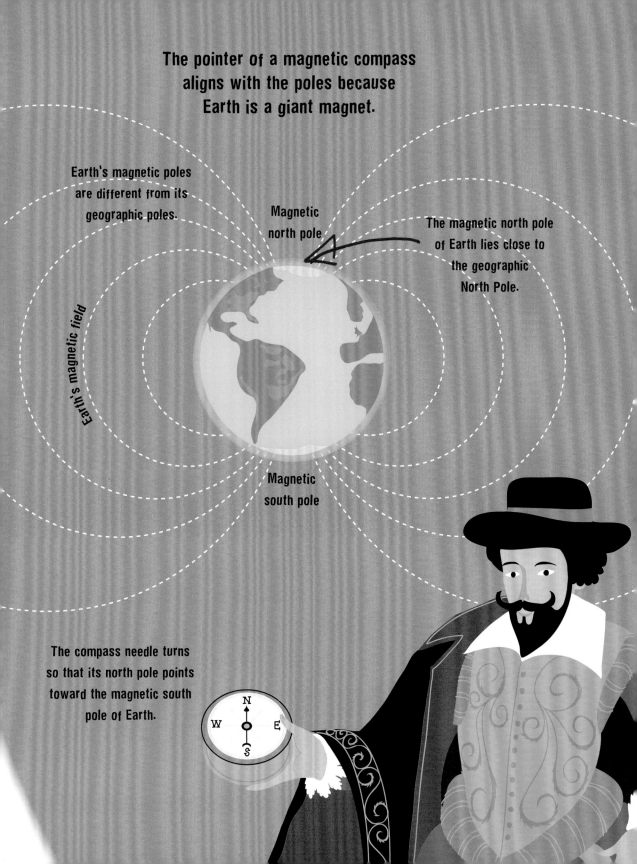

The pointer of a magnetic compass
aligns with the poles because
Earth is a giant magnet.

Earth's magnetic poles
are different from its
geographic poles.

Magnetic
north pole

The magnetic north pole
of Earth lies close to
the geographic
North Pole.

Earth's magnetic field

Magnetic
south pole

The compass needle turns
so that its north pole points
toward the magnetic south
pole of Earth.

Motion

... in 30 seconds

Centuries ago, scientists were fascinated by motion. It seemed obvious that you need to keep pushing or pulling an object for it to continue moving. For example, horses have to pull carts. You have to push a wheelbarrow along the ground. But what keeps pushing an arrow through the air, or a pendulum from side to side?

Galileo

Galileo realized that what seemed obvious was wrong. Moving objects don't need pushing or pulling to keep them going unless something else is constantly slowing them down. Carts need horses to overcome the friction of the ground and the drag of the air. In space, with no ground or air, a horseless cart would never stop moving—much as the moon keeps moving around Earth.

Galileo also investigated the motion of a pendulum. He found that a pendulum swings from side to side in a time that depends only on its length. This "pendulum law" made it possible to use pendulums to make clocks keep good time.

3-second sum-up

Motion only changes when force is applied.

3-minute mission Pendulum Law

You need: • Large metal nut • Plastic cord at least 20 inches (50 cm) long • **An adult helper**

Tie the nut to the plastic cord. Hold the cord about 16 inches (40 cm) above the nut and start it swinging. Without moving the hand that holds the cord, pull the cord's free end to shorten the pendulum. The swings will speed up. Experiment with different weights and angles to see what happens.

Objects only need to be pushed or pulled to keep them in motion if there is a force slowing them down.

Without continuous pulling or pushing, the cart will stop.

The horse and cart move steadily along.

The air creates some drag.

The ground creates some friction.

With no ground or air to create drag, the cart will keep moving without being pushed or pulled.

Cells

... in 30 seconds

One of the most important laws of biology says that all living things are made of tiny units called cells. The simplest creatures have only a single cell. Even in complex animals like humans, individual cells behave in some ways like separate creatures. Most have a core in the center called a nucleus, which controls the cell, and each pulls in food chemicals and pushes out waste.

We are built from many different types of cells, and each has a job to do. Muscle cells get shorter so we can move. Bone cells are strong and hard, providing the body's framework. White blood cells move around on their own, destroying enemy cells that invade the body.

Because cells are so small, they were only discovered after the microscope was invented. The first person known to have seen cells was Robert Hooke in 1665. The first cells he saw were dead ones in a piece of cork. He called them "cells" because they reminded him of the tiny rooms in which monks lived.

Robert
Hooke

3-second sum-up

Every living thing is made of cells.

3-minute mission Watch Cells at Work

You need: • 2 glasses • Salt • 1 carrot • Warm water

1 Fill two glasses halfway with warm water. Stir several spoonfuls of salt into glass 1.

2 Put half a carrot in each glass, cut end down. Let sit overnight.

3 The carrot cells will "try" to make the saltiness of the water inside them match the saltiness outside. In glass 2, plain water flows into the cells, reducing their saltiness and making them plump and swollen. In glass 1 (with salt), water from the carrot cells flows out, making the cells collapse and the carrot shrivel.

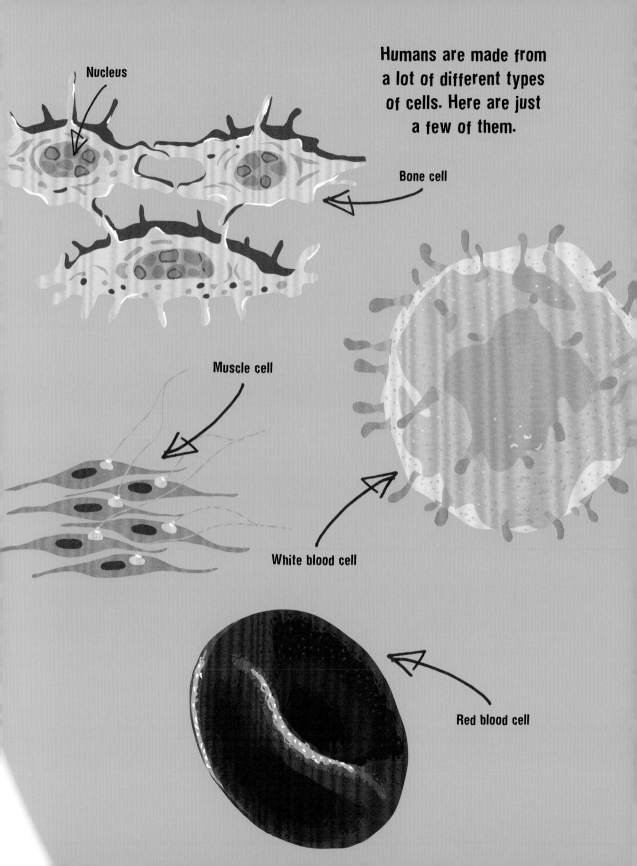

Nucleus

Humans are made from
a lot of different types
of cells. Here are just
a few of them.

Bone cell

Muscle cell

White blood cell

Red blood cell

Gravity
... in 30 seconds

The ancient Greeks were certain that Earth and the rest of the universe were made of different things and obeyed different laws. In the sixteenth century, scientists such as Galileo questioned this idea. The view emerged that the same laws work all over the universe.

Isaac Newton decided that the same law made apples fall to the ground and kept the moon close to Earth: the law of gravity. Gravity attracts objects in space toward each other and pulls objects on Earth toward the center of the planet, so that things fall to the ground when they are dropped.

Newton worked out a mathematical version of his discovery and used it to predict the motion of the moon, comets, and planets. Today, it is used to steer spacecraft through the solar system and beyond.

Isaac Newton

3-minute mission Find Your Center of Gravity

Newton found that gravity acts as if all the mass of an object is gathered together at its "center of gravity," with the mass of the object arranged evenly around it. For a sphere like Earth, this is in the core in the center. For us, it depends how we arrange our limbs. You can find your own center of gravity:

Stand against a wall with your heels touching it. Drop a coin about 12 inches (30 cm) in front of you. Can you pick it up without moving your feet or bending your knees? You couldn't? That's because your center of gravity moved away from the wall until it was no longer over your feet. With nothing under it, your center of gravity started to fall, and so did you.

3-second sum-up

Gravity is a force that pulls objects toward each other.

Light
... in 30 seconds

Isaac Newton was such an important scientist that many of his colleagues thought he must be right about everything. They agreed with him that light must be made of particles (tiny lumps), too small to see separately.

But not everyone thought that way. To Christiaan Huygens, a Dutch scientist, it seemed more likely that light travels in waves, and he used this idea to explain many of its properties.

By the beginning of the nineteenth century, most people thought that Huygens was right. Many things were much easier to explain if light was made of waves, including Newton's own discovery that white light is made of different colors. It was thought that the various colors differ only in the length of their waves.

Christiaan Huygens

Now we know that light is more complicated than either Newton or Huygens believed. It often does behave like a wave, but at other times it behaves as if it is made of tiny lumps. Scientists now understand that light is made of photons, which are neither waves nor particles.

3-second sum-up

White light is a mix of different colors, and all light travels in straight lines.

3-minute mission See a Spectrum

All you need for this is a sunny day and a CD. Place the CD face-down in a sunlit place like a windowsill, and look at it. You should see a rainbow of colors on the surface—if not, move your head around until you do.

When Newton shone light through a
glass prism, he found that it split into
a mixture of colors.

When the light strikes the
glass at an angle, each
color bends.

The light waves travel
toward the triangular
glass prism.

Long-wavelength red light
waves bend the least.

Short-wavelength
violet light waves
bend the most.

Age of Reason

In the eighteenth century, the idea of using "reason"—logical thought—took hold in Europe and led to additional scientific developments. This period is called the Enlightenment, or the Age of Reason, because it shone the light of science onto the world.

Age of Reason
Glossary

atom A tiny object made of a number of even tinier particles. Atoms link together to make all the things we see around us.

carbon dioxide A gas that forms part of the air. We breathe it out and it is made when things burn.

chemical reaction A process by which one set of substances changes into a different set.

electron A tiny particle. Atoms contain electrons.

element A substance that cannot be divided into simpler substances. Gold and iron are both elements.

energy The thing that makes things happen. Motion, light, sound, and heat are all kinds of energy, and there are many others.

hexagon A flat shape with six straight edges and six corners.

kinetic To do with motion.

magnetic field The area around a magnet where objects are pulled by it.

neutron One of the particles that is found in the nucleus of an atom.

nucleus (plural: nuclei) The core in the center of something, such as a cell or an atom.

oxygen A gas in the air that we need to breathe.

particle Any tiny lump of matter too small to see. Atoms are particles, and so are electrons.

pressure The amount of force that acts over a particular area. If you press your thumb hard onto a corkboard, it might make a shallow dent. If you press your thumb hard onto a drawing pin, the pressure is concentrated in the point, enough to push it right into the cork.

proton One of the particles found in the nucleus of an atom.

quark The particle from which neutrons and protons are made.

spectrum (plural: spectra) A rainbow-like smear of light. Spectra can be used to find out about bright objects such as stars.

Kinetic Theory

... in 30 seconds

Of all the many scientific theories, there is none more successful than the kinetic theory of gases. "Kinetic" means "to do with motion." This theory says that gases behave as if they are made of tiny particles in constant motion, endlessly bouncing off each other.

For instance, if a sealed box of thin metal is heated, it soon explodes. This is because heating the gas in the box makes its particles move faster, so they hit the sides of the box harder and harder, until the box bursts.

This theory helps us understand heat, too. The difference between hot and cold water is that the molecules move faster in hot water. The heat you feel from hot water comes from the molecules striking your skin.

One scientist who helped to develop kinetic theory was Daniel Bernoulli. His work explains how planes fly.

Daniel
Bernoulli

3-second sum-up

Gases are made of tiny particles in constant motion.

3-minute mission
Air-pressure Experiment

You need: • Two 12-inch (30-cm) lengths of string • 2 table tennis balls • Piece of wood • 1 straw • Books

1 Tape a string to each ball. Tape the other ends to the wood, so the balls hang ½ inch (1 cm) apart.

2 Support the wood on piles of books. Try to move the balls apart by using the straw to blow between them.

3 You'll find they move together. Just as in a plane's wing, the reduced pressure of the fast-moving air is the reason they move.

The difference in air pressure above and below a plane'

Faster air exerts less pressure than slower air. The air above the wing doesn't press on it as strongly as the air underneath.

The air passing over the wing travels faster than the air passing underneath it.

The wing is specially shaped to make the air travel faster over the top than the bottom.

The stronger air pressure below the wing pushes the plane upward.

Spectroscopy

... in 30 seconds

In the early nineteenth century, people thought it would never be possible to find out what the stars were made of. But within a few decades, they knew—thanks to the spectroscope.

A spectroscope splits up light into a spectrum, which often looks like a rainbow. It spreads out the mixture of colored lights given out by a star, so they can be seen separately. The first person to make a spectroscope was Thomas Melville.

Thomas Melville

Each element that makes up a star produces different wavelengths of light. Scientists can measure the different wavelengths of the light to tell what the stars are made of.

Spectra can also tell scientists about the mass, speed, spin, temperature, pressure, and magnetic field of stars. They are used to study materials on Earth, too.

3-second sum-up

Spectra tell us what stars are made of.

3-minute mission Make a Spectroscope

You need: • An old CD • Strong adhesive tape • Cardboard tube • Thin cardboard pieces

1 Press tape strips firmly over the CD's upper side. Pull off the strips to remove some of the CD coating.

2 Tape the CD to one end of the tube. Now, cut out a cardboard circle a little bigger than the end of the tube, then cut an oblong hole in it and tape it to the other end of the tube. Take two cardboard pieces just bigger than the hole. Tape them down so each covers half the hole, leaving a narrow slit between them.

3 Place the CD-end close to your eye. Point the tube at light sources. Incandescent bulbs give a complete spectrum. Try fluorescent lights, street lights, and neon signs. Some give bands of color that come from elements in gases in the lights.

Scientists can use a spectroscope to study the light waves of stars and find out what they are made from.

Starlight is focused on a prism.

The spectroscope separates the light into a spectrum.

It makes a pattern of colors on a photographic plate.

Astronomers can tell which elements the star is made of from this pattern.

Carbon

Oxygen

Iron

Nitrogen

Chemical Reactions

... in 30 seconds

Inside your body right now, food chemicals are being changed to sugars and other chemicals to give you energy. These changes release a gas called carbon dioxide, which you breathe out. You breathe in oxygen, which is used to release energy from more food chemicals.

A similar process happens when wood or coal is burned. Oxygen is taken in, combined with carbon from the wood or coal, and given out as carbon dioxide gas. In both digestion and burning, one result is heat. The link between oxygen and burning was first discovered by scientist Antoine Lavoisier in the 1770s.

Antoine Lavoisier

Chemical changes are happening all around us all the time. Controlled chemical reactions give us many things, from plastics to candies. The changes may release or take in heat, which can be more useful than the chemical products themselves.

3-second sum-up

Chemical reactions change one set of substances into another.

3-minute mission **Chemical Explosion**

You need: • 3 tablespoons baking soda • Paper towel • 1 cup warmed vinegar • Sandwich bag • **An adult helper**

Don't get the liquid in your eyes. It's harmless, but will sting!

1 Do this outdoors. Spoon the baking soda onto the paper towel and fold the towel up around it.

2 Pour the vinegar into the bag. Drop the paper towel in.

3 Quickly seal the bag and move away. The bag will burst messily a few seconds later. A chemical in the vinegar reacts with the baking soda to produce water, sodium acetate, and carbon dioxide gas. The gas bursts the bag.

Propane is a fuel used to make hot-air balloons rise.

When propane is ignited, the resulting chemical reaction makes it take in oxygen and release much more heat.

The carbon and hydrogen in the propane react with the oxygen. They change into carbon dioxide and water and release heat and light.

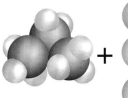 + →

Propane
C_3H_8

Oxygen gas
$5\ O_2$

Carbon dioxide
$3\ CO_2$

Water
$4\ H_2O$

Heat and light

This is the chemical formula showing the reaction.

Atoms

... in 30 seconds

This book is made of atoms. So are you, and so is everything you can see. But atoms are much too small to see. The period at the end of this sentence is about 10 million times wider than an atom.

Leucippus and Democritus, two Greeks who lived more than 2,500 years ago, were the first to believe in atoms. However, it was not until about 200 years ago that the chemist John Dalton discovered evidence of them.

John Dalton

Dalton found that the behavior of different chemicals could be explained by the idea that each element they contained was made of one kind of atom.

Dalton thought that atoms were hard, unbreakable lumps. In fact, each atom has a tiny hard core called a nucleus, with layers of much-lighter particles called electrons around it. The nucleus is made of two kinds of particles: neutrons and protons. These particles are made of even tinier particles called quarks. As far as we know, quarks cannot be broken down into anything smaller.

3-second sum-up

All matter is made of invisible atoms.

Dalton's Discovery Explained

It's possible to make two gases from carbon and oxygen. One is poison, and the other is harmless. It takes exactly twice as much oxygen to turn the carbon into the harmless gas as the poisonous one. Dalton realized that this means that every molecule of the harmless gas contains two atoms of oxygen (plus one of carbon), while the poison gas molecules each contain one atom of oxygen (plus one of carbon). So, the way elements combine shows they must be made of atoms.

Everything is made of atoms. Today, we know what atoms are made of.

All matter can be divided into smaller and smaller units.

Except for the smallest units—atoms.

The ancient Greeks were the first to believe in atoms. Hundreds of years later, chemist John Dalton progressed this idea.

Dalton realized the atoms of an element—such as carbon—were all the same.

He believed that each atom was an unbreakable lump.

Now we know that atoms have a nucleus made of neutrons and protons, with electrons around it.

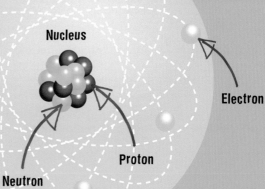

Nucleus

Atom

Neutron

Proton

Electron

Modern Industry

From the late eighteenth century on, a number of new inventions, many of them using steam power, led to great developments in technology. Modern industry began. People realized that science was not only a way of finding out about the world, but it could also provide much better machines—which meant their owners could make more money.

Modern Industry
Glossary

amino acid A type of chemical from which proteins are made.

atom A tiny object made of a number of even tinier particles. Atoms link together to make all the things we see around us.

atomic number The number of protons per atom that an element contains.

bacterium (plural: bacteria) A tiny living thing with just one cell. Some bacteria cause illnesses, such as food poisoning, tetanus, and whooping cough.

compass An instrument used by travelers to find which direction they are going in. A compass contains a long, thin magnet that is free to turn around. This always lines up so that its ends point to the North and South poles of the Earth.

DNA Short for deoxyribonucleic acid. DNA typically exists as large molecules, found inside cells. It contains the information needed for a body to grow.

dynamo A device that uses magnets to make electricity from motion. Often, the motion is that of running water, wind, or steam, which turns a wheel on the dynamo. Dynamos are often called generators, because they generate (make) electricity.

electric motor A device that uses a magnet to make an electric wire move. Motors are usually built to make a wheel spin.

electromagnet A device in which electricity moves around a coil of wire to turn a metal rod into a strong magnet. When the electricity stops, the magnetism disappears.

electron A tiny particle. Atoms contain electrons.

element A substance that cannot be divided into simpler substances. Gold and iron are both elements.

energy The thing that makes things happen. Motion, light, sound, and heat are all kinds of energy, and there are many others.

evolution The process by which new kinds of animals and plants develop from earlier kinds. Evolution is usually a very slow process, taking many generations to cause changes that can be noticed.

fungus (plural: fungi) A type of living thing that gets its food from the things it grows on. Mushrooms are one kind of fungus. Tiny fungi cause a few human illnesses and most plant diseases.

gene A section of DNA that carries instructions for the manufacture of proteins by the cell. Proteins are very important for building bodies.

germ A bacterium, virus, or fungus that can cause illness.

mass The amount of stuff there is in something. On Earth, the more mass a thing has, the more it weighs.

trait Something that may be passed from parents to children, such as eye color, left-handedness, or freckles.

virus A very tiny, very complicated type of chemical that behaves like a simple living creature. Many illnesses are caused by viruses, including measles, flu, and cold sores.

Electromagnetism

... in 30 seconds

In the early nineteenth century, scientists found that electricity can move magnetic compass needles. In 1831, Michael Faraday managed to use electricity to make a magnet—called an electromagnet.

He also built the world's first electric motor (a machine that uses electricity and magnetism to make something move) and the first dynamo (which turns motion into electricity).

Today, most technology depends on Faraday's discoveries. Electric motors can be found in almost every vehicle, in drills and other power tools, and in moving toys.

Michael Faraday

Almost all the electricity we use comes from dynamos. They are found in wind turbines and power stations, and are even used to power bike lights. Powerful electromagnets are used in scrap yards, in medical scanners, and in the machines used by scientists to investigate atoms.

3-second sum-up

Faraday invented machines that turn electricity and magnetism into motion.

3-minute mission Make an Electromagnet

You need: • Thin, plastic-coated wire • Large screwdriver • 4.5v battery • **An adult helper**

1 Wind the wire around the screwdriver, making at least 50 turns.

2 Leave at least 12 inches (30 cm) of wire free at each end.

3 Ask an adult to expose the last 1 inch (2 cm) of the wire ends.

4 Connect the ends to the terminals of the battery. The screwdriver will become an electromagnet. It will attract some metal objects, such as paper clips.

Faraday used electricity and magnetism to build the first motor and dynamo.

In Faraday's disk dynamo, the magnet makes electricity from the copper disk.

The electricity goes along the wire to the meter and back to the disk.

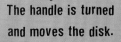

The handle is turned and moves the disk.

The pointer shows how much electricity is made.

Dynamos or electric motors are found in these modern machines.

Energy

... in 30 seconds

Energy is what makes things happen. It comes in many forms, including motion, light, electricity, magnetism, sound, and heat. Which forms of energy are being used where you are right now?

In the nineteenth century, scientists worked out that energy comes in many different forms and can change from one form to another. They realized that when one form of energy seems to disappear—for example, when a sound dies away—it hasn't really gone away. It has changed to another form.

This idea had great practical uses. During the nineteenth century, machines were built to make clothes and other goods. Steam engines moved the goods around. The job of engines and machines was to change energy from one form to another. For example, in a steam engine, the chemical energy of coal is changed to the motion of the train. The new science of energy helped the inventors to get the maximum motion from every ton of coal.

3-second sum-up

Energy makes everything happen.

How Energy is Transformed

Have you ever taken off a sweater in a dark room? You see a glow and hear crackling. These effects are caused by energy changes. Your muscles change chemical energy from your blood into motion energy as you move your arms. This motion makes electrical energy as the sweater is dragged over you. The electrical energy changes into the light and sound energy you see and hear. This works best when the air is dry, which is usually in the winter.

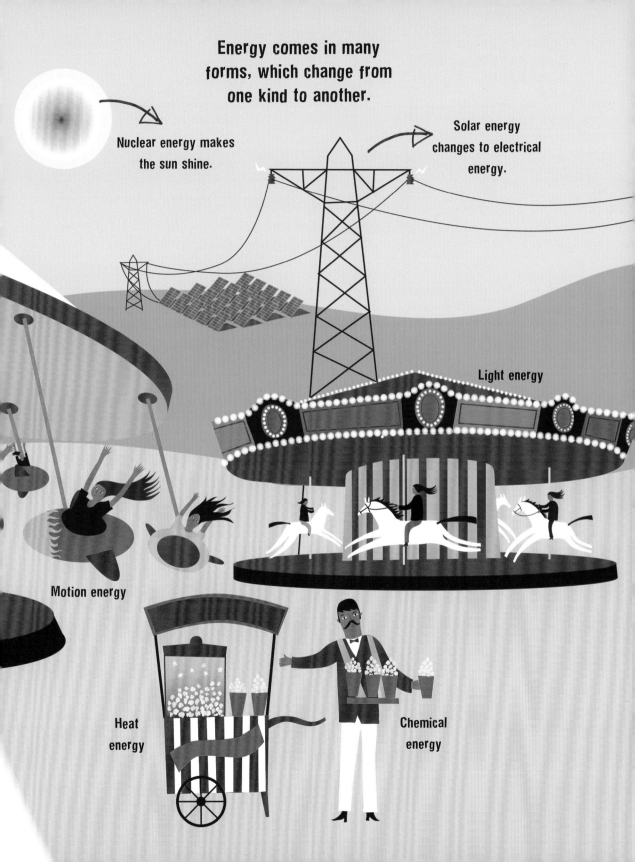

Energy comes in many forms, which change from one kind to another.

Nuclear energy makes the sun shine.

Solar energy changes to electrical energy.

Light energy

Motion energy

Heat energy

Chemical energy

Evolution

... in 30 seconds

In the nineteenth century, most Christians thought that God had made humans, plants, and animals just a few thousand years ago, and that they had not changed since. But in 1859, Charles Darwin showed that, in fact, living things had been around for much longer. And today's versions look completely different from their ancestors.

Darwin's discovery is called evolution. It starts with two facts:

1. Living things increase in numbers until there is too little food left for them all. Then they starve or fight for what remains.

2. Every living thing is a little different to its parents and siblings.

Charles Darwin

If a creature is born with a difference that gives it an advantage over its siblings—such as sharper teeth—it will win the fight for food and have a better chance to survive and go on to breed. Its children may inherit the advantage and survive, too. Those without the advantage eventually die out. So, over generations, the bodies of creatures evolve (change).

3-second sum-up

The living things on Earth evolved over millions of years.

3-minute mission Camouflage

Animals evolve camouflage to make it harder for enemies to see them. Compete with a friend to find camouflaged "prey."

Each of you has half the backyard or playground, three envelopes of treats, and coloring pens. Your friend has five minutes to find three hiding places, color an envelope to "camouflage" it, and hide it there. You're next. Then search for each other's envelopes. Whoever finds them quickest, wins!

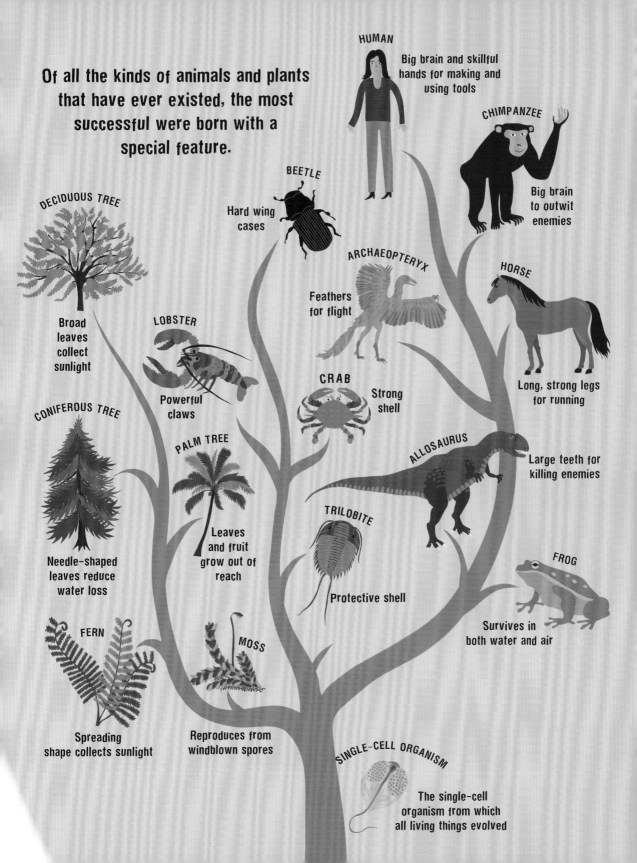

Of all the kinds of animals and plants that have ever existed, the most successful were born with a special feature.

HUMAN
Big brain and skillful hands for making and using tools

CHIMPANZEE
Big brain to outwit enemies

BEETLE
Hard wing cases

DECIDUOUS TREE
Broad leaves collect sunlight

ARCHAEOPTERYX
Feathers for flight

HORSE
Long, strong legs for running

LOBSTER
Powerful claws

CRAB
Strong shell

CONIFEROUS TREE
Needle-shaped leaves reduce water loss

PALM TREE
Leaves and fruit grow out of reach

ALLOSAURUS
Large teeth for killing enemies

TRILOBITE
Protective shell

FROG
Survives in both water and air

FERN
Spreading shape collects sunlight

MOSS
Reproduces from windblown spores

SINGLE-CELL ORGANISM
The single-cell organism from which all living things evolved

Germs

... in 30 seconds

Today, if we're sick, we expect a doctor to make us better. Yet just a few centuries ago, the "medicines" that were available often made the patient worse. To cure an illness, you need to know what causes it, but people in those days didn't have a clue.

Louis Pasteur helped to change all that. In the mid-nineteenth century, he proved that germs cause diseases, and every disease has its own type of germ. Diseases could be cured by killing the germs.

Pasteur also showed that germs cause the decay of food and that heat could kill those germs. This was very useful. For example, people learned to heat milk to make it safe to drink.

Now we know that some "germs" are tiny living creatures called bacteria. Some are fungi (tiny relatives of mushrooms) and some are viruses—complicated chemicals that behave like living things.

Louis Pasteur

3-second sum-up

Germs cause diseases.

3-minute mission **Grow Your Own Germs**

You need: • Potato • Knife • Fork • 3 sandwich bags • **An adult helper**

1 Wash your hands, then cut three equal slices of potato.

2 Use a clean fork to place slice 1 in a sandwich bag. Seal the bag and label it "control."

3 Spit on slice 2. Seal it in a sandwich bag and label it "spit."

4 Wipe slice 3 on the ground. Seal it in a sandwich bag and label it "ground."

5 Put all three bags in a dark cupboard for one week. Then look at them. The one with the most germs should look the most different. The "control" slice should look the least changed.

Pasteur proved that germs cause
diseases and make food decay.
He also showed that heat
can kill some germs.

Some germs
cause disease.

Germs are everywhere
but you cannot see them.

Others cause
food to go bad.

Pasteurization kills germs.

Heat kills the germs
in the milk.

The milk is cooled.

The milk is now
safe to drink.

Genetics

... in 30 seconds

You probably think it's obvious that you look a little like your parents. But why is this? Why do we look more like one parent than the other? Why don't brothers look exactly the same?

Now we know that the answers lie deep inside our cells. The "plans" of our individual bodies—how they look and how they work—are held in chemical patterns called genes. The genes of babies contain a mixture of genes from their parents. They inherit traits from each parent.

Gregor Mendel

In the nineteenth century, Gregor Mendel worked out the main laws of inheritance—long before genes were discovered. Yet he found how they worked by carrying out an enormous number of experiments on pea plants. He bred different types and worked out mathematically the rules that showed the chances of inheriting particular traits. Unfortunately, Mendel's work was ignored until after his death.

3-second sum-up

Genetics is the study of how characteristics are passed on.

3-minute mission Traits Contest

Make about ten score cards, each with six check boxes. Write an inherited trait (see below) on each card and put the cards in a bag.

Attached earlobes	Can roll your tongue
Freckles	Dark hair
Gets hay fever	Naturally curly hair
Cleft chin	Dimples
Left-handed	Food allergy

Traits score card

1
2
3
4
5
6

Invite your family and friends to play, giving each a score card and pen. Draw a card from the bag and read it out. Any player who has the trait on the card checks a box. The person with the most traits wins.

In many plants and animals,
about one-quarter of a generation will
have a particular trait (such as blue eyes)
while the rest do not. This is why.

Mother

Bb

Father

Bb

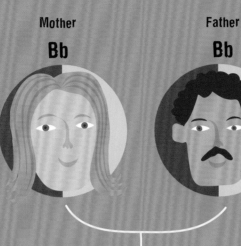

Each person has a pair
of genes that decide eye
color, and each gene has
two forms. If both genes
are type "B" or one is "B"
and one is "b," the eyes
are brown.

BB

Bb

Bb

bb

This child has inherited
two B genes. Eyes
are brown.

These two children have each
inherited one B gene and one b gene.
B genes are stronger than b genes,
so they have brown eyes.

This child has inherited two
b genes. This is the only way
of having blue eyes.

Periodic Table

... in 30 seconds

By the 1860s, more than 50 elements had been found and the weights of their atoms roughly measured. Chemists noticed that when the elements were listed in order of atomic weights, those with similar properties turned up at regular intervals. But the patterns were unclear.

It was Dmitri Mendeleev who made the breakthrough that revealed the true pattern of the elements. He realized that there might be elements still to discover.

Mendeleev grouped elements with similar properties together and left gaps to keep the order of the pattern clear. The result was the periodic table, which is vital to chemists today.

Dmitri Mendeleev

In the periodic table, all elements in the same column (group) have similar properties. In each group, the properties of the elements change gradually. In Group 1, all the elements react with water, each more violently than the one above. Group 8 elements hardly ever react with anything.

3-second sum-up

The properties of the elements form a natural pattern.

Eight Extraordinary Elements

The number shows the element's position in the periodic table.

Hydrogen (1): Most common element in the universe and in you
Helium (2): Makes your voice squeaky if you breathe it
Carbon (6): Makes more compounds than all the other elements put together
Iron (26): What Earth is mostly made of
Gallium (31): Metal that melts in your hand
Arsenic (33): Deadly poison
Mercury (80): Liquid metal (at room temperature)
Copernicium (112): Disappears within a few minutes of being made

The periodic table

The periodic table is arranged in groups of elements with similar properties.

This column is Group 1 and contains the alkali metals. These elements have strong reactions.

The last column (Group 8) contains the noble gases. All of these elements are odorless, colorless, and very stable.

Helium is used to make balloons float.

Argon is used in lightbulbs.

Xenon is used in lighthouses.

Lithium

Sodium

Potassium

Rubidium

Caesium

Francium

Sodium

Turns white in air, fizzes in water.

Caesium

Bursts into flames in air; explodes in water.

Helium

Neon

Argon

Krypton

Xenon

Radon

Ununoctium

Modern Science

By the end of the nineteenth century, scientists thought they understood the universe, but a few areas were still unexplained. Meanwhile, improved science education allowed for more people to become scientists. These scientists found that many of the most basic scientific ideas about the world were wrong. A new period of discovery began.

3·8

Modern Science
Glossary

amino acid A type of chemical from which proteins are made.

atom A tiny object made of a number of even tinier particles. Atoms link together to make all the things we see around us.

electron A tiny particle. Atoms contain electrons.

energy The thing that makes things happen. Motion, light, sound, and heat are all kinds of energy, and there are many others.

evolution The process by which new kinds of animals and plants develop from earlier kinds. Evolution is usually a very slow process, taking many generations to cause changes that can be noticed.

fossils Remains of animals or plants that lived millions of years ago.

gravity The force that holds you to the ground and causes things to fall. It keeps the Moon moving around Earth, and Earth moving around the Sun.

neutron A tiny particle in the nucleus of an atom.

nuclear To do with the nuclei (the cores in the center) of atoms.

nuclear fission A process in which the nuclei of large atoms break apart, releasing a great deal of energy. Nuclear power stations use nuclear fission to make electricity, and nuclear fission is also used in some powerful bombs.

nuclear fusion A process in which the nuclei of small atoms join together, releasing a great deal of energy. The Sun and other stars use nuclear fusion to make light and heat, and nuclear fusion is also used in the most powerful bombs.

nucleus (plural: nuclei) The core at the center of something, such as a cell or an atom.

protein A substance made from tiny building blocks called amino acids. Proteins are a vital part of all living things.

proton One of the particles found in the nucleus of an atom.

quantum (plural: quanta) A tiny lump of energy. A photon is a quantum of light.

relativity A theory explaining how time, space, and gravity are related.

spectroscope An instrument used to split up the light from a glowing object, such as the Sun, a star, or a hot gas, into a spectrum.

universe Everything that exists.

The Quantum

... in 30 seconds

At the end of the nineteenth century, one of the basic ideas of science said that tiny objects are just small-scale versions of the things we see around us. For instance, atoms were like tiny, hard balls.

But this common-sense idea was wrong. In fact, the small-scale world is very different from our own. At the beginning of the twentieth century, physicists began to discover just how strange that world really is.

They discovered that just as matter exists in tiny lumps called atoms, energy (such as light) also exists in tiny lumps, called quanta.

Atoms contain electrons. Sometimes an electron will get rid of energy in the form of a tiny flash of light. But the electron can only lose one quantum of energy at a time, so those tiny flashes are always exactly the same brightness (and they are always the same color, too).

3-minute mission Go Dotty

We don't notice quanta because they are so tiny, a little like the way pictures made of dots look normal at a distance.

Take four soft-tip pens in red, yellow, blue, and black. On white paper, draw a picture of some orange and lemon trees under a blue sky with white, gray, and black clouds. Do this using only dots!

Tip: Yellow and red dots side-by-side make orange at a distance; blue and yellow make green; and black with gaps (on white paper) makes gray.

Electron

An electron releases energy as a tiny flash of light (a photon), one Quantum at a time.

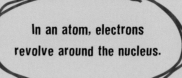

In an atom, electrons revolve around the nucleus.

Nucleus

As its energy increases, the electron moves to a different position in the atom.

As it returns to its lower energy state, the electron releases a Quantum of light, a photon.

The photon has left the atom. This process happens many times, and each time the photon has exactly the same color and brightness.

Nuclear Energy

... in 30 seconds

In the early twentieth century, scientists added a new kind of energy to the list of those they knew about: the energy locked up in the nuclei (cores) of atoms.

When fuel burns, a chemical reaction produces heat and light energies. When atoms in the fuel separate from each other and join up in new combinations, energy is released. The nuclei of the atoms are not involved in this process.

The heat and light of the Sun are produced in a different way. The nuclei of hydrogen atoms are crushed together to form the nuclei of helium, and this releases light and heat. This process is called nuclear fusion.

Nuclear power stations use another process, called nuclear fission. High-speed particles called neutrons smash into enormous nuclei of the element uranium. These nuclei fall apart, releasing more neutrons and plenty of energy.

3-second sum-up

Atomic nuclei are packed with energy.

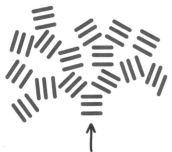

Push this one over first.

3-minute mission
Make a Chain Reaction

Stand dominoes in a branching pattern as shown to the left, seen from above. To make sure you don't start the reaction accidentally before you're ready, leave a few gaps until you have placed the rest. Then push over the first domino. The number of falling dominoes and the noise they make increases—just as the number of splitting nuclei and the energy they release increase in a nuclear chain reaction.

Nuclear fusion and nuclear fission both produce energy.

In the Sun, the nuclei of atoms are crushed together to form the nuclei of helium, releasing light and heat. This is nuclear fusion.

Energy

Neutrons

Neutron

Uranium nucleus

Nucleus starts to split

In nuclear fission, very large atoms are broken apart to form smaller ones.

Nuclear power stations use nuclear fission to produce energy.

Relativity

... in 30 seconds

By 1900, scientists thought they understood the universe. Then a scientist called Albert Einstein came up with a theory that if a spacecraft traveled at thousands of miles per second, strange things would happen to space and time.

If you could watch the craft as it rushed past, you would see it change shape and look squashed. You would also see that everyone onboard was moving in slow motion. And you could measure that the craft was much heavier than when it took off.

Stranger still, if someone on the spacecraft looked out at you, they would see the same things. You would look squashed, you would move in slow motion, and you would be heavier, too.

Albert Einstein

Einstein called his theory relativity. It states that the shapes, masses, and other properties of objects change according to how they are measured. He showed that very heavy objects, such as the Sun, affect time and space. If you could stay on the Sun for a few years, you would return home to find that time had passed more slowly for you. You might now be younger than a friend born after you!

3-second sum-up

Relativity explains how time, space, and gravity work.

3-minute mission Squashed Spacecraft

You need: • A notebook with plenty of pages • Felt pen

1 Draw a side-on spacecraft in the top right corner of every right-hand page. Make each one shorter than the one before.

2 Hold the book in your left hand and bend back the top right page corners with your thumb.

3 Flick the pages to see the spacecraft fly. It will gradually squash like a real one would if it traveled fast enough.

Emily is on a spacecraft traveling at 93,000 miles (150,000 km) a second. Before she set off, she and Jack both set their clocks to zero.

Einstein's theory tells us that if something travels fast enough, its measurable properties will change.

It takes her 3.8 minutes by her clock to reach Jack's teeny planet. As she races past she sees only 3.3 minutes have passed on the planet.

3·3

3·8

3·3

On Jack's planet, the clock and Jack's watch both say 3.8 minutes have passed by the time Emily's spacecraft flies by. But the clock on the spacecraft's side reads just 3.3 minutes.

3·8

Continental Drift

... in 30 seconds

It's hard to imagine your country drifting off to another part of the world. Because this idea is so strange, Earth's history was not understood until the twentieth century.

If you look at a map of the world, you can see that some of the continents could fit together neatly. By the 1910s, several scientists had noticed this. Alfred Wegener also noticed that fossils that had been found on distant continents were amazingly similar.

Wegener decided that the continents must have been joined together long ago in a supercontinent. This was named Pangaea. The animals and plants of the time could have lived in areas that are now split up into today's continents.

Alfred Wegener

No one believed Wegener until it was found that the continents each exist on a vast stone "plate." The plates extend out beneath the sea so there are no gaps between them. They float on a huge area of liquid rock, and are all moving very slowly.

3-second sum-up

The continents are slowly moving.

3-minute mission
Moving Continental Plates

This experiment shows that continental plates move even though there are no gaps between them. Take two thin doormats or small rugs to be continental plates. Lay them side by side on a smooth surface and push them hard against each other. What happens? As on Earth, one plate may slip under another, both may rise up, or they may buckle. Buckling and rising cause mountains on Earth, and all these effects can cause earthquakes and volcanic eruptions.

The theory of continental drift explains that there was once just one large supercontinent.

Wegener found that several far-apart places on Earth contained the same kinds of fossils.

Cynognathus

Mesosaurus

Lystrosaurus

Glossopteris

This could be explained if those places had once been side by side, exactly as the continental drift theory said.

Life Chemistry

... in 30 seconds

In 1924, a Russian scientist called Alexander Oparin made a startling suggestion. What if we (and other living things) are actually enormously complicated structures of chemicals, which evolved over billions of years from simple everyday chemicals?

Many people—especially those with strong religious views—strongly disagreed. Few believed Oparin at the time. However, a U.S. scientist named Harold Urey did. He worked out that the chemicals on Earth billions of years ago really could have developed in this way, using the energy of lightning to do so.

One of Urey's students tested the idea. He mixed simple chemicals in his laboratory and exposed them to electrical sparks. The results were amazing. All kinds of chemicals found in living things formed, including amino acids—the building blocks of all life on Earth.

Alexander
Oparin

3-second sum-up

All life evolved from chemicals.

3-minute mission
Extract a Protein

You need: • 2 cups milk • 2 tablespoons clear vinegar • Fine-mesh strainer • Paper towels • **An adult helper**

1 Ask an adult to heat the milk until it is steaming. Stir in the vinegar. Let the now-lumpy mixture cool. The lumps are the protein, casein.

2 Line the strainer with paper towels, then pour the mixture into it so the liquid drains off.

3 Pour the casein onto a stack of paper towels. Press more paper towels on top to dry it.

4 You can color the casein with food colors and mold it—knead it well first. It will take about two days to set hard.

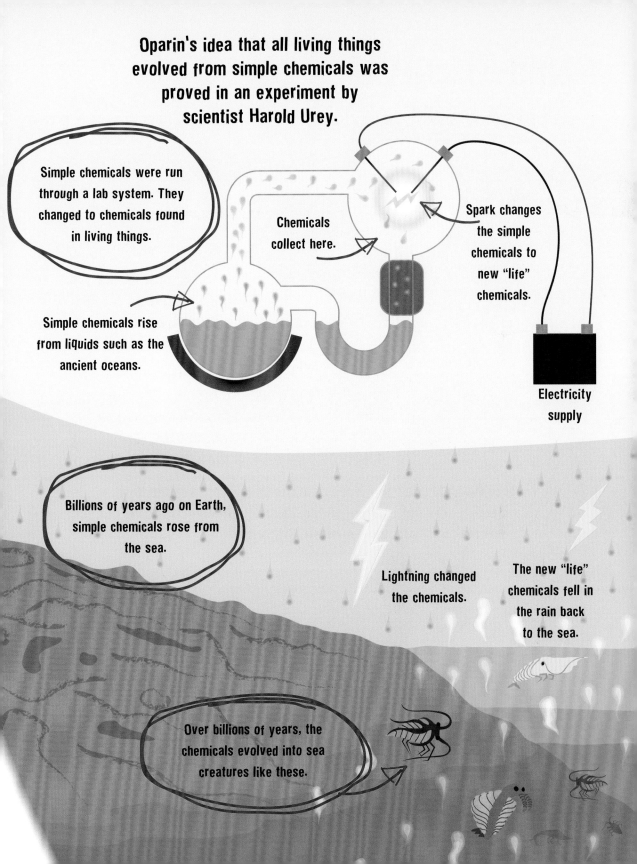

Uncertainty

... in 30 seconds

The quantum world of tiny things is very different from the human-scale world we live in.

We are used to the idea that an object, such as a football, has an exact size, weight, and position. But electron-sized things don't—they only have rough positions.

Imagine standing within a high wall, built all around you in a circle. If it's too smooth to climb, too hard to break, too high to jump over, and too deep-set to tunnel, you will be there forever.

But not if the rules of the quantum world applied! In that world, everything about you is only roughly defined, including height, strength, and position. That means you could escape. You might suddenly be in a position beyond the wall, have the strength to break through, or the height to step over it.

It sounds unbelievable, but this is the only way to explain how particles can escape from atoms. They do not have the power to break out, but every so often, they DO!

3-second sum-up

At a tiny scale, there are few exact values.

3-minute mission Uncertain Objects

You need: • Cardboard potato chip tube • Candle • **An adult helper**

1 Ask an adult to cut a 1-inch (2.5-cm)-wide hole in the lid of the tube.

2 Ask the adult to light a candle. Blow it out after one minute.

3 Hold the open end of the tube over the wick to catch the smoke. Lift up the tube and put the lid on. Squeeze the tube gently to make smoke rings. These are like huge versions of electrons.

4 Try finding their edges. Even counting them may be impossible!

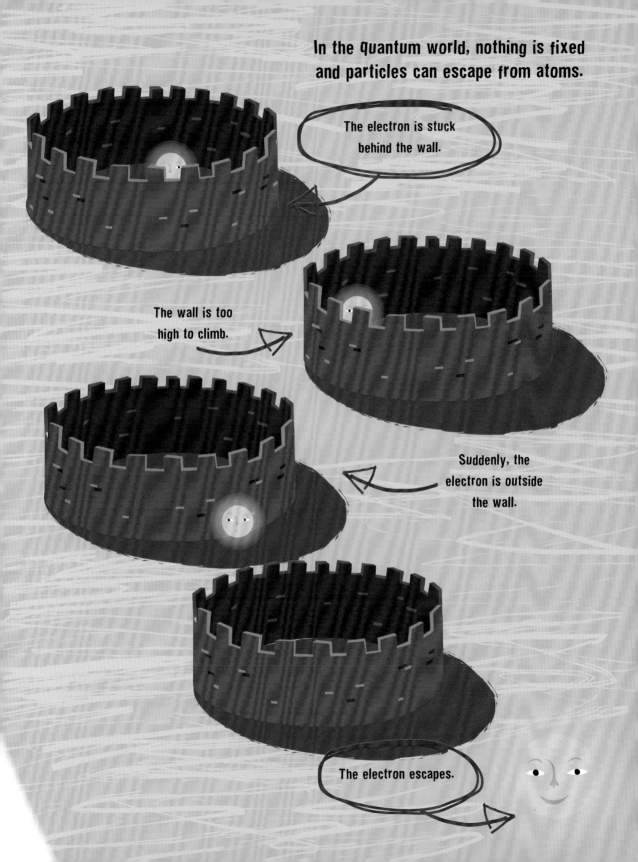

Science Now

Science and technology played an important role in World War II (1939–1945), which led to more money being spent on research and education. Now scientists could work together in international teams. This era of "big science" has led to new breakthroughs.

Science Now
Glossary

amino acid A type of chemical from which proteins are made.

atom A tiny object made of a number of even tinier particles. Atoms link together to make all the things we see around us.

base One of the four main chemicals that make up DNA.

DNA Short for deoxyribonucleic acid. DNA typically exists as large molecules, found inside cells. It contains the information needed for a body to grow.

electron A tiny particle. Atoms contain electrons.

energy The thing that makes things happen. Motion, light, sound, and heat are all kinds of energy, and there are many others.

gene A section of DNA that carries instructions for the manufacture of proteins by the cell. Proteins are very important for building bodies.

gravity The force that holds you to the ground and causes things to fall. It keeps the moon moving around Earth, and Earth moving around the Sun.

mass The amount of stuff there is in something. On Earth, the more mass a thing has, the more it weighs.

molecule Two or more atoms joined together. Water is made from molecules, each of which was made by joining two atoms of hydrogen with one of oxygen.

nucleus (plural: nuclei) The core at the center of something, such as a cell or an atom.

particle Any tiny lump of matter too small to see. Atoms are particles, and so are electrons.

protein A substance made from tiny building blocks called amino acids. Proteins are a vital part of all living things.

spectroscope An instrument used to split up the light from a glowing object, such as the sun, a star, or a hot gas, into a spectrum.

universe Everything that exists.

The Big Bang

... in 30 seconds

About a century ago, several astronomers noticed something odd. They had discovered a way to measure how fast an object in space is moving away. The light from the object becomes very slightly redder. They used this to measure the speed at which galaxies were moving.

The scientists found that the farther these distant galaxies were, the faster they were moving away from us. This means that the whole universe is expanding.

Since the parts of the universe are moving apart, they must have once been close together. They were thrown apart in a huge burst of energy long ago—this burst of energy is now called the "big bang." In 1948, a scientist called George Gamow worked out how a big bang could form the atoms we know about today.

George Gamow

3-second sum-up

The universe began as a sudden expansion called the big bang.

3-minute mission Bread Universe

You need: • 4 cups bread mix • Handful of raisins • Large bowl • Plastic wrap • **An adult helper**

1 Make up the bread mix. Add the raisins. Each raisin represents a cluster of galaxies.

2 Knead the dough on a floured surface until smooth. Place in the bowl, cover with plastic, and let rise for an hour.

3 The raisins will each move away from the rest as the dough expands, just as clusters of galaxies move apart as space expands.

4 Knead again, let expand for half an hour, then bake for about 30 minutes in a preheated oven at 400° F, until the bread sounds hollow when tapped. Like the universe, it starts off hot but soon cools down.

The universe started with a burst of energy called the big bang. This idea came from the discovery that the galaxies are moving apart.

The universe formed about 13,700 million years ago. It was very small and very hot.

The universe started to expand very quickly and then cooled down.

As it got cooler, light atoms formed.

Atoms joined together to make heavier atoms, stars, and planets.

DNA

... in 30 seconds

One day in 1953, two scientists named James Watson and Francis Crick burst into a quiet Cambridge pub (an English bar) and declared, "We've just discovered the secret of life!"

And so they had. After several months, they had worked out the structure of the chemical from which all life is built. Called deoxyribonucleic acid (DNA), the chemical is huge and very complicated.

It has to be: Every one of the trillions of DNA molecules in your body contains a complete set of instructions for building you from chemicals.

Nearly everything around us is made of molecules, which are built from atoms—usually just a few atoms per molecule. But DNA contains around 200 billion atoms joined to make a long strip. If the strip was straight, it would be several inches long. But it has to fit inside the nucleus of the cell, which is only several thousandths of an inch wide.

James Watson and Francis Crick

So it is coiled up tightly in a double-helix shape. It is this shape that Watson and Crick had worked out, using a special image of DNA obtained from another scientist, Rosalind Franklin.

3-second sum-up

DNA contains the instructions to make living things.

How Does DNA Copy Itself?

Most body cells have short lives, so new ones are regularly made. To do this, an old cell splits in half. The new cells each need their own DNA, so DNA in the old cell splits into a pair of new DNA molecules. DNA is a like a zipper, with two rows of joined-up nucleotides acting like the two rows of teeth. To split, the DNA unzips itself, so the two rows of "teeth" become separated. New "teeth" (nucleotides) lock onto the unzipped parts of DNA and make new DNA.

All life is made from the complex chemical DNA. The sequence is slightly different for every person, except identical twins.

Adenine

Cytosine

Thymine

Guanine

DNA is made up of nucleotides, which can include one of four types of base—adenine, cytosine, guanine, and thymine.

The bases pair up in a long twisted chain called a double helix.

This is DNA.

Genetic Modification

... in 30 seconds

The pairs of bases in a DNA molecule work like the letters of a very simple alphabet. Just as a long series of letters makes a sentence, so a long series of these pairs makes a gene. And, just like a sentence, a gene is an instruction—for example, "Color the eyes blue." A DNA molecule is a long series of genes, like an instruction book is a long series of sentences.

It is possible to remove genes from the DNA of one living thing and insert them into the DNA of another. This is like cutting some instructions from one book and pasting them into another. Once the new version of the DNA "instruction book" is used, a different type of the living thing will result.

This cutting and pasting is called genetic modification (GM). GM has been used to make bacteria that produce medicine, plants that glow in the dark when they need watering, and crops that resist disease.

3-second sum-up

GM makes new kinds of living things.

3-minute mission Extract Your Own DNA

You need: • Small paper cups • Bottle of colorless sports drink • Liquid soap • Pineapple juice • Wooden toothpick • Alcohol (ethanol) • Jar with a lid • **An adult helper**

1 Put the alcohol in the freezer 24 hours beforehand. Then swish the sports drink in your mouth for 2 whole minutes. Spit into the cup. Then pour it into the jar until it is one-third full.

2 Add soap until the jar is halfway full. Gently turn the jar to mix. Add a few drops of pineapple juice and mix again.

3 Carefully add a little alcohol so it floats on top.

4 Twirl the toothpick around the white gooey material near the top—your DNA!

Cutting and pasting DNA from a firefly into leaf cells forms a new glow-in-the-dark plant.

Firefly glow genes are shot into a plant by a gene gun.

A special "glow" gene makes the firefly glow.

Pieces of the plant containing the glow genes are removed.

The seedlings grow into plants with glow genes in every cell.

Seedlings are grown from the pieces of plant.

The Standard Model

... in 30 seconds

The "Standard Model" is the name given to the best theory of the universe we have today. It says that everything is made from 17 kinds of particles. Four of these particles are linked to three kinds of forces in the universe. The fourth and most familiar force is gravity.

The standard model has a lot to say about "fields." When a magnet is moved close enough to a piece of metal to pull on it, we say that the metal is "in the magnetic field" of the magnet.

When an object in space is close enough to Earth to be pulled by Earth's gravity, we say that the object is inside Earth's gravitational field.

This theory can explain almost everything that happens in most areas of science. But it can't explain gravity properly.

3-minute mission Battling Forces

You need: • 4 inches (10 cm) cotton thread • Large paper clip • Adhesive tape • Magnet

1 Tie the thread to the paper clip. Tape the other end to a table.

2 Lift the paper clip until the thread is straight and vertical. Hold a magnet just above the paper clip.

3 Let go, and the clip should hang upward in space. Move the magnet slowly upward. The magnetic field around the paper clip will become weaker until it is weaker than the gravity field of Earth. At that point, gravity will win the battle of the forces and the clip will fall down.

3-second sum-up

The standard model is our best theory of the universe.

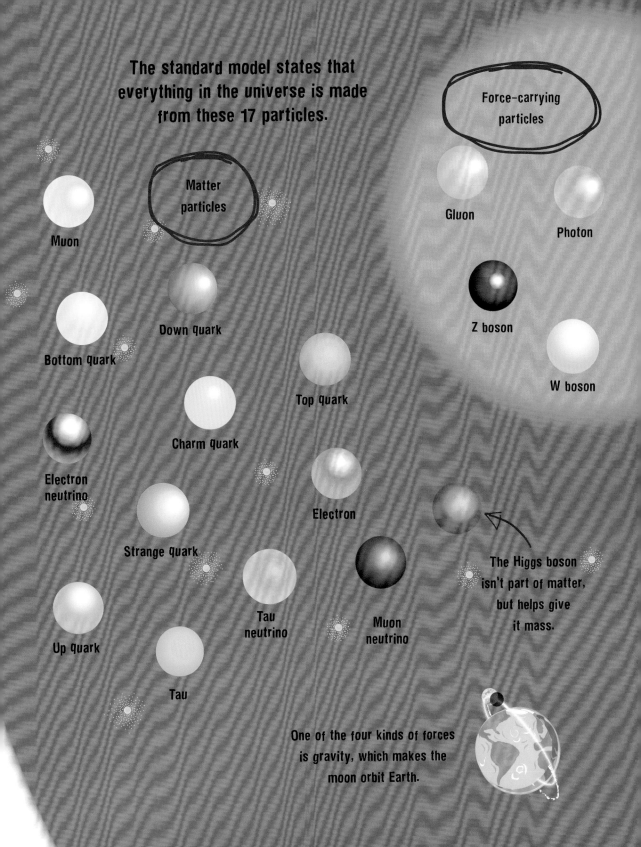

String Theory

... in 30 seconds

The current theory, the standard model (see pages 88–89) cannot explain gravity. String theory can—but the theory is not finished, so it does not work properly yet!

String theory explains that the 17 kinds of particles are made of "string." But it's not like the normal string we use. Each piece is so tiny that not even the most powerful scientific instruments in the world could see one.

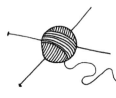

The idea is that these tiny strings are constantly vibrating (wobbling), a little like guitar strings. But they can vibrate in many ways. The strings that different particles are made from vibrate differently. The four forces, including gravity and electromagnetism, are also made of these vibrating strings.

No one knows for sure if string theory is right. If it is, it will be the first theory that successfully explains everything in the universe.

3-second sum-up

Everything may be made of "string."

3-minute mission Show String Theory

In string theory, a particular string can vibrate only in certain ways—like real strings.

1 Hold one end of a jump rope and ask a friend to hold the other end. Make the rope move up and down to make a loop.

2 Move your hand faster to make a double loop.

3 You might be able to move faster and make a triple loop.

4 Try to make a pattern with 1½ loops. You can't. This "string" can only vibrate in certain ways.

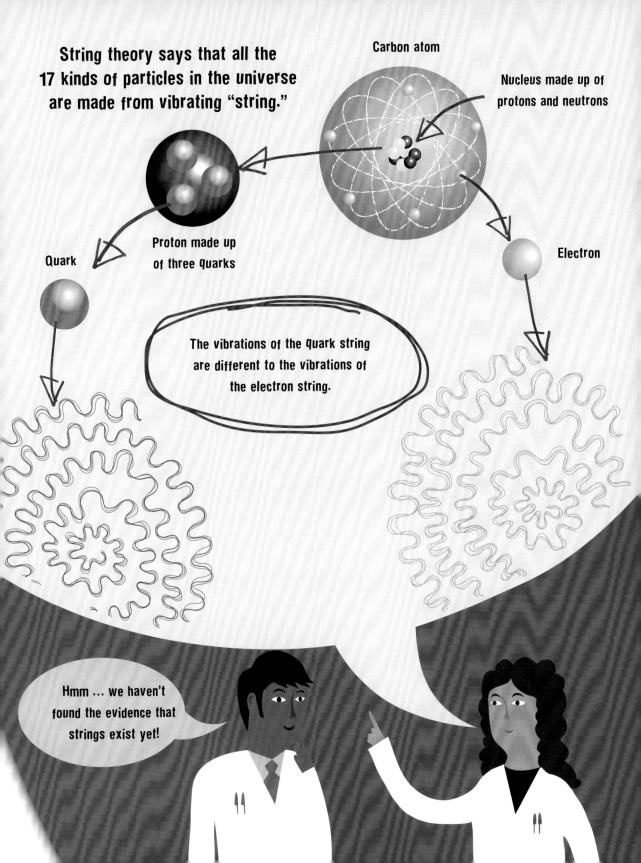

Discover More

FICTION

Einstein: The Girl Who Hated Maths by John Agard
Hodder Children's Books, 2013

NONFICTION BOOKS

1001 Inventions and Awesome Facts from Muslim Civilization by National Geographic
National Geographic Kids, 2013

Albert Einstein and Relativity for Kids by Jerome Pohlen
Kindle Edition, 2012

Ancient Science: 40 Time-Traveling, World-Exploring, History-Making Activities for Kids by Jim Wiese
Wiley, 2003

Big Ideas That Changed the World by Dorling Kindersley
Dorling Kindersley, 2013

Galileo for Kids: His Life and Ideas, 25 Activities by Richard Panchyk
Kindle Edition, 2005

History for Children: Einstein for Kids by Ian D. Fraser
Kindle Edition, 2013

It's Elementary! Putting the Crackle into Chemistry by Robert Winston
Dorling Kindersley, 2010

Space in 30 Seconds by Clive Gifford
Sandy Creek, 2014

Tools of the Ancient Greeks by W. Eric Martin
Nomad Press, 2006

What's the Big Idea? by Vicki Cobb
Sky Pony Press, 2013

DVDs—suitable for all ages

The Gene Code by Dr. Adam Rutherford
The Open University/BBC, 2011

Wonders of the Solar System by Brian Cox
2entertain, 2010

WEB SITES

Explore the Solar System
https://spaceplace.nasa.gov/solar-system-explorer/en/
Discover more about the Solar System

Fun Science Experiments and Activities
https://www.natgeokids.com/discover/science/nature/science-experiments-for-kids/
Experiments to try at home

Science Experiments You Can Do At Home or School
http://www.sciencebob.com/experiments/
Instructions for experiments and explanations of how they work

Science Games for Kids: Forces in Action
http://www.sciencekids.co.nz/gamesactivities/forcesinaction.html
Activities to show how forces work

Science Kids at Home: Genetics—What are Genes?
http://www.sciencekidsathome.com/science_topics/genetics-a.html
How genes work

APPS

Kid Science: Physics Experiments by Selectsoft Publishing
Selectsoft Publishing, 2011

Index

Index